Poetry for the New Millennium
Volume VI

Migraines and Their Remedies

by

Sandra de Helen

2023

Disclaimer

Neither the publisher nor the author is engaged in rendering professional medical advice or services to the reader. The statements made about products and services have not been evaluated by the U.S. Food and Drug Administration. The ideas, suggestions, and procedures provided in this book are for informational purposes only and are not intended to diagnose, treat, cure, or prevent any condition or disease.

The information presented does not constitute any health or medical advice. Please seek advice from your healthcare provider for your personal health concerns prior to taking healthcare advice from this book. Neither the publisher nor the author shall be held liable or responsible for any loss or damage allegedly arising from any suggestion or information contained in this book.

The author and publisher are providing this book and its contents on an "as is" basis and make no representations or warranties of any kind with respect to this book or its contents. The author and publisher disclaim all such representations and warranties, including for example warranties of merchantability and healthcare for a particular purpose. In addition, the author and publisher do not represent or warrant that the information accessible via this book is accurate, complete, or current. Please consult with your own physician or healthcare specialist regarding the suggestions and recommendations made in this book.

Advance Praise for Migraines and Their Remedies

Sandra de Helen's newest book is a one-of-a-kind collection of poems about the experience of living with migraines. Each poem is accompanied by a remedy—sometimes pharmaceutical and often herbal and word-of-mouth, suggestions offered by a friend or fellow sufferer. Throughout this delightful volume, de Helen's humor filters through the pain. Her use of personification to characterize an approaching or disabling migraine is skillful and allows the reader to get inside the monster's "head." "Saturday Night Date" and "Whatever It Takes" are two of my favorite poems in the collection. There's something here for everyone—sufferer and sympathizer. This book, illustrated by black and white drawings, will make a unique addition to your poetry collection.
~Sandra Anfang, nationally acclaimed author of poetry collections *Finishing School; Looking Glass Heart;* **and** *Road Worrier: Poems of the Inner and Outer Landscape.*

Being a migraineur, having a child who suffers even more severely, I felt every word, every phrase, EVERY poem deeply, and have a few new remedies to consider.
~Mercedes Lewis, Poet, author of *Glimpses of a Fractured Soul*

Sandra de Helen infuses her new poetry collection *Migraines and Their Remedies* with humor. Having suffered through years of migraines, de Helen masterfully describes the unwanted visitor's "blinding pain" with a twist. Even through moments of debilitating pain, the migraine is muse, "bad company"—a companion that "will have to order in, I hope it has its own credit card." de Helen's ability to stab at pain playfully demonstrates her unique voice and power as poet.
~ Cherie Gough, Freelance Contributor at *HuffPost*

Written to honor those who suffer from migraines, Sandra de Helen's book sheds light on the mystery of this intense pain, and the many remedies tried to relieve suffering. Her poems describe in exquisite detail how migraines feel as she is having them. They offer a compassionate, honest and fascinating look into these unwelcome visitors, and how writing of their pain helped free her poetic voice.
~Sarah Rohrs, poet, **newspaper reporter refugee and educator**

It seems I've always been *aware* of the existence of grizzly bears and also the debilitating effects of migraine headaches. My awareness of the former told me I shouldn't ever be in the same place at the same time with a huge bear…okay, not even a small one. My awareness of the latter told me zilch about the life-controlling power of migraines. Then, I read this collection of poetry.

Sandra de Helen's poems, the slightly humorous and ironic ones as well as those roiling in pain, take the reader beyond an *awareness* of this malady. They deliver the *reality* of people who experience this disease, try to abate its pain, and persist under its unceasing efforts to control their lives.
~**Renée Bess, award-winning novelist, poet, essayist, and short story writer**

There are few topics more difficult to write about than one's own chronic physical pain, but Sandra de Helen does so with vivid imagery, vulnerable transparency, and flashes of wit and wisdom. *Migraines and Their Remedies* gives readers a window to see both the lows—falling like heavy brow blows—and the heights to which pain warriors will climb to reach for relief, and how just in rising again and again, the poet knows that she is the winning champion.
~**Bethel Swift, poet**

Except as specifically stated in this book, neither the author or publisher, nor any authors, contributors, or other representatives will be liable for damages arising out of or in connection with the use of this book. This is a comprehensive limitation of liability that applies to all damages of any kind, including (without limitation) compensatory; direct, indirect or consequential damages; loss of data, income or profit; loss of or damage to property and claims of third parties.

You understand that this book is not intended as a substitute for consultation with a licensed healthcare practitioner, such as your physician. Before you begin any healthcare program, or change your lifestyle in any way, you will consult your physician or another licensed healthcare practitioner to ensure that you are in good health and that the examples contained in this book will not harm you.

This book provides content related to physical and/or mental health issues. As such, use of this book implies your acceptance of this disclaimer.

Copyright

A Launch Point Press Trade Paperback Original
Migraines and Their Remedies is a work of poetic fiction. Names, characters, places, and incidents are either the product of the author's imagination or are used fictitiously. Any resemblance to actual persons living or dead, business establishments, events, or locales is entirely coincidental.

Copyright © 2023 by Sandra de Helen

All rights reserved. Launch Point Press supports copyright which enables creativity, free speech, and fairness. Thank you for buying the authorized version of this book and for following copyright laws by not using or reproducing any part of this book in any manner whatsoever, including Internet usage, without written permission from Launch Point Press, except in the form of brief quotations embodied in critical reviews and articles. Your cooperation and respect supports authors and allows Launch Point Press to continue to publish the books you want to read.

ISBN: 978-1-63304-057-1
Ebook: 978-1-63304-058-8

FIRST EDITION: First Printing, 2023

Editing: Jodi Zeramby, Lori L. Lake
Copyediting/Proofreading: Jodi Zeramby
Book and Cover Design: Peggy Zeramby

Portland, Oregon www.LaunchPointPress.com

Table of Contents

Author's Foreword

Dedication

1. Migraine
2. Migraine Wake-Up Call
3. Surgery
4. Bad Company
5. Migraine senryu
6. Midnight Migraines
7. Migraine Againe
8. Migraine Haiku
9. Saturday Night Dance
10. Whatever it Takes
11. Monster
12. The Spiral Staircase
13. Hold Back the Dawn
14. Two-Day Headache Binge

15. Migraine Day Three

16. Another Headache Poem

17. The Lost Weekend

18. To M

19. Little Visits

20. Migraines Might Slow You Down

21. A True Story

22. The Worst

Afterword

About the Author

Other books in Poetry for the New Millennium series

Author's Foreword

Migraines Made Me a Better Poet

Poetry struck me before I was diagnosed with migraine headaches. I don't remember when I wrote my first poem. My mom and dad both wrote poems regularly, and I grew up believing it was something everyone did. As necessary to daily life as reading books.

In high school, my English teacher Mrs. Wallace encouraged me to write more, and she showed me how to edit and polish what I wrote. Thanks to her support, I published my first poem when I was fourteen.

I gave up writing poetry in my mid-twenties, at around the time I began to have "sick headaches," and ten years before migraines began to make themselves a regular part of my life. I stopped writing after a male college professor told me my poetry was no good because I didn't write like a man. I don't blame him for the headaches, but his words certainly contributed to my self-doubt.

I began writing daily in my forties. I wrote plays, short stories, but never a poem. I didn't believe I could write poetry, but I felt confident about my plays and short stories.

At first, the migraines came only twice a year. Over time, they became frequent enough I was making regular trips to the emergency room, and seeing my neurologist more often than my internist.

After years of preventive medication, rescue pain relief, changes in my diet, additions to my exercise routine, and trying every possible migraine remedy I heard or read about, the migraines became chronic, and I was at their mercy every other day, sometimes for days at a time.

My writing suffered even more than I did.

After trying one remedy, which entailed drawing my headaches, I realized all the drawings looked almost the same. One day I remembered the art I'm best at uses words as its medium. I began to write migraine poems.

Given the frequency of the headaches, I wrote a lot of migraine poems.

The accepted wisdom is if a person spends ten thousand hours practicing their craft, they will master it. If true, I am indeed a master migraineur.

What is true for me is that by writing migraine poems even when I was incapable of writing other poetry, or writing anything else at all, I was honing the craft of poetry.

Unlike the drawings I made of my headaches, the poems became more nuanced, better at metaphor, included symbolism, and had meaning beyond the experience of pain. I went from writing about the pain to describing the migraines as a stalker, a jealous lover, a heartless guardian. I wrote about headache experiences and found they reminded me of other experiences in my life. I wrote in different formats such as haiku and senryu.

Writing while under the influence of pain taught me how to block other distractions, how to hone in on making my work better no matter what life tossed me.

I had given up writing poetry after one bad experience. Years of writing while experiencing intense pain allowed me to return to the craft, to call myself a poet once again.

(Published by *Folks Magazine* under the title "How Chronic Illness Helped me Perfect my Craft.")

Dedication

To all the migraineurs of the world.

Migraine

Conventional wisdom says pain
is a gift. Something provided us
by deities to help us understand
our bodies, to force us to rest,
to lead us to living in the moment.

A friend says too much living
in the now leaves us no room
to daydream. No room for reflection
on times past. None of us is truly
capable of perpetual presence.

So please tell me, goddess who inflicts this white hot
pain to my head,
is my current sacrifice of two days every week
enough for you?
If those hours are not sufficient
to fill my quota,
may I sacrifice my life? Now?

Remedy #1
When you want to die from a migraine, treat the headache as you would depression.

Sandra's Rx: Go for a walk.
Getting outdoors, no matter the weather, is good for you. Go for the maximum amount of time you are able given the current circumstances. Dress appropriately, and add sunglasses.

Migraine Wake-up Call

A small beep, a muffled
ring of the phone, all
deep within the folds of
the sleep of dawn.

One eyelid opens, sees gray
of day, too early. Closes
tight. Sleep descends.

Public bus rolls by half
a block away, overloaded
with morning commuters.

Rain hits the skylight,
relentless as the hungry
cat pacing the floor
less than one meter
from my head.

I am awake. I am up.
I wonder about that
beep, that call. No one,
nothing.

Why am I up so early?
Within minutes the
answer is clear.

My head is throbbing
with pain,

familiar
stabbing
pain.

No time to fully
awaken, have my
tea, settle in
to morning.

This day
belongs to
Migraine.

Remedy #2
From my friend Anne:

In terms of a cure, well…but in my heavy migraine days, when I sensed the event early enough, some ibuprofen and either caffeine or feverfew tea could help. It didn't take it away but made it more manageable.

Anne's Rx:
Catch the migraine early. Ibuprofen, 400 mg every four hours. Caffeine or feverfew tea.

Surgery

Surgeons must be very careful
When they take the knife!
Underneath their fine incisions
Stirs the culprit, — Life!
~Emily Dickinson

Survivor of several bouts
with surgeons, while under anesthesia
I, not he—the surgeon was always he—-
I sometimes wish for more surgery.

The clean cutting away of the body's
problem, the knowledge afterward
I once again survived.

If only all the body's problems
could be so simply
resolved.

I'd go under the knife one more time,
if surgery would remove the
migraines.

Remedy #3
From my friend Kathleen S:

Mine stopped when I had my ovaries removed. At times the migraines were bad enough to send me to the hospital to control pain. What worked best for me before my ovaries were removed: Cafergot. It can be toxic, but I used it for years without side effects and relief within twenty minutes.

Occasionally I now have the aura without pain. Strong coffee helps.

Kathleen's Rx:
Have your ovaries removed. [This does not work for cis-gendered males. It also did not work for the poet.] Cafergot: Take 200 mg at the start of attack; 100 mg additional every half hour, if needed, for full relief (maximum six tablets per attack, ten per week).

Bad Company

Every July since 1999, I get company
on the first of July. It stays all month.
It sneaks out for a day or two
here and there, but never has specific plans,
so I have to stay at home,
waiting on it hand and foot
as it sits on my head,
pounding, squeezing, sometimes
poking me in the eye, kicking me
in the gut, jabbing me in the side
of my head. Migraine.

Sure it lives here year-round,
but not every freaking day like it does
each July. One June for instance, migraine
was here only nine days
holding me hostage.
January it kept me down for ten,
March for fifteen.

But so far this month, I've managed
to free myself from its vice only
a few days, and only one of them
in the last eight. I can't even get out
to buy groceries to feed
the damned thing. It will
have to order in.
I hope it has its own credit card.

Remedy #4
From fellow migraineur Nik:

I have migraines up to twenty-two days per month if I don't regularly have a slew of shots, including an epidural and Botox.

None of the cures work for me on their own. A combination of rizatriptan or Imitrex with ALL of the following: Gatorade, half an energy drink, nausea medication, a mild muscle relaxer, Tylenol, and Benadryl. This combo works almost every time, though sometimes only for a few hours.

To be fair, I have a spinal injury which triggers most of my headaches.

Nik's Rx: Epidural, Botox, Gatorade, half an energy drink, nausea medication, a mild muscle relaxer, Tylenol, and Benadryl. ALL of them. [The poet herself does not recommend this, as it sounds like a possible overdose.]

Migraine senryu

My head hurts way too much
to work or write or even
go to the doctor.

Remedy #5
From my friend Kathleen H:

Migraine update: After being free of migraines for the better part of a year, I started to get them again a few months ago. More and more frequently, seemingly inexplicably. The good news is I figured out that by taking half a teaspoon of salt with water at the onset of aura, I could avoid about 90 percent of migraine symptoms once the aura passed.

This led me to a new internet search about using electrolyte balance to get rid of a migraine. There are people who have done the research! I found a Facebook group dedicated to this practice, which offers a free download of their book on the Stanley Migraine Protocol, where I learned the VAST majority of people who adhere to these protocols have been able to drastically reduce or get rid of migraine.

After chatting with the author of the book, it occurred to me the licorice tea I had been taking for POTS symptoms is known to deplete/deregulate potassium. I stopped it immediately and HAVE NOT HAD A MIGRAINE SINCE.

Another fascinating discovery: Sugar (including many starches) can cause a dramatic change in the sodium/potassium ratios in your body. This is one of the reasons a ketogenic diet has been such a positive addition to my life.

If you suffer from migraines, I highly recommend checking out the Stanton research on migraine. There is a Facebook page and their free downloadable book (which is REALLY long, and I haven't gotten through it, yet). Search for the Stanton Migraine Protocol.

Kathleen's Rx: Salt, one-half teaspoon, dissolved in water. Drink the salt water at onset of migraine aura.

Midnight Migraines

What's this? A booty call? I'm
getting into bed when you have
the nerve to come knocking?

Where you been? It's Saturday night;
you were busy all night out, carousing
with who knows who, doing who knows what.

You got some gall coming up in here
at this time of night. All right, stop
with the bright lights and all that noise.

I can see I'm not gonna have any
peace from you. Give me that glass
of water and those pills.

Now get out of here
and leave me the hell alone.
You make me sick.

Remedy #6
From my friend Lisa:

I no longer get migraines, but I used to lie on the bed
in a darkened room with a heating pad wrapped
around my head.

Lisa's Rx: Lie on a bed in a darkened room with a
heating pad wrapped around your head.

Migraine Againe

Twice in one week after three
weeks without a single one.
Sometimes they fall this way.

Other times they like to huddle
around each other like kittens
suckling their mama, my brain
one giant belly of teats.

Today's headache sent a scout,
a foot soldier with a bayonet
to repeatedly stab my liver first

to make sure I awakened
and arose from my warm bed,
breakfasted, and planned my day
before throwing everything at my head.

Surprise attack! Yes! We got her,
gentlemen, we are taking her
down. Molten rivers sluice across my head

as I fall back against my chair,
my eyes unable to open against
even this gray afternoon

now that my forehead is in the
grip of your tiny warriors,
pulling at every tendon.

I reach for my pills, unable to

12 Migraines and Their Remedies

find them by sound, less able
to read the labels than I could have

if only I had
surrendered when I heard
the first bugle cry instead
of bravely struggling to my
writing desk to die while
booting up.

Remedy #7 Use ice.

Sandra's Rx: Put an ice pack on your forehead, scalp, or neck to get pain relief. Experts aren't sure exactly why it works, but reducing the flow of blood might be part of it. You can also try a frozen gel pack or a washcloth that you've rinsed in cold water.

Migraine Haiku

One more migraineur
turns her face from the sunshine,
prays for quiet spring.

Remedy #8 Yoga

Sandra's Rx: Try any of the following yoga poses:
Cat and cow pose
Seated forward fold
Ragdoll pose
Downward dog
Legs up the wall
Bridge pose
Savasana

Saturday Night Dance

Dancing with lightning, bright
blue flashes behind my right eye
deep in my brain around
my right ear and back
so fast, faster than the speed of
lightning—bright pain.

Deep dark oil slick pain sliding
around crevices as though
they were dead man curves
on Route 66 hoping for a
semi daring herself.

Semi trying to make it home to
Sugar Mama, hitting the slick,
missing the curve,
seeing nothing but that
last flash of light before
darkness overtakes.

I am that driver, the waiting
widow, the eight-year-old
child hearing the crashing
semi.

I am blue lightning
on Saturday night.

Remedy #9 From the Mayo Clinic: Find a calm environment.

At the first sign of a migraine, take a break and step away from whatever you're doing if possible.

· **Turn off the lights.** Light and sound can make migraine pain worse. Relax in a dark, quiet room. Sleep if you can.

· **Try temperature therapy.** Apply hot or cold compresses to your head or neck. Ice packs have a numbing effect, which may dull the pain. Hot packs and heating pads can relax tense muscles. Warm showers or baths may have a similar effect.

· **Sip a caffeinated drink.** In small amounts, caffeine alone can relieve migraine pain in the early stages. Caffeine also may enhance the pain-reducing effects of acetaminophen (Tylenol, others) and aspirin.

Be careful, however. Drinking too much caffeine too often can lead to withdrawal headaches later on. And having caffeine too late in the day may interfere with sleep, which can affect migraines.

Mayo Clinic's Rx: Find a calm environment, turn off the lights, try temperature therapy, and sip a caffeinated drink.

Whatever it Takes

I am willing to live without corn
and all its products for the rest of my life.

I am willing to dance naked
under the light of the moon
on the mountain in the rain.

I will bury a new potato
on the path to the outhouse.
I will soak my head in a tub of butter.

I will eat fifteen servings of colorful veggies
every day and twice on Sunday.
I am willing to follow the advice
of every relative and friend, even Facebook
friends I've never met.

I swear to you I am willing
to try every remedy there is
to rid myself of migraines.

All but one: I refuse to pound
nails into my head.

Remedy #10 Holes in the head.

Sandra's Rx: Regarding putting holes in one's head: I, the poet, once had a physically disabled client who had gone outside the country to have holes drilled in her head to try to alleviate migraine pain. She asked if she should tell the judge (who was to determine her disability eligibility). I advised her not to. I admired her persistence in pursuing pain relief, but I believed the judge might think she was a mental rather than a physical disability case. Unfortunately, the holes in her head did not work, and neither did her attempt to get disability benefits.

About this one "cure" I haven't tried: There is speculation that the age-old practice of trepanation, i.e. a surgical intervention in which a hole is drilled or scraped into the human skull, was to alleviate the swelling of the brain of a wounded soldier. Maybe so, but those of us who suffer migraine headaches believe it was also an attempt to relieve migraine pain. I doubt it was successful.

Monster

Stalker. Abuser. You've caused me
more pain that any relationship
I've ever willingly entered into in my life.

Let the record show I did not
invite you into my body, my mind,
my psyche. You are not wanted here.

I've asked you to leave in every way
I know how. Begged, pleaded,
ignored.

I've doped up, nearly killed myself
—all to no apparent avail. Will it be until death
do us part without the benefit of marriage?

I divorce thee! If only one could
separate herself from migraine by
jumping backward over a broom.

Remedy #11
From my friend DJ:

Among the more natural remedies is the herb feverfew. Taken in capsule form every day, with whatever other vitamins you may take, feverfew builds up to help prevent migraines. I no longer get migraines at all (they miraculously stopped when I left my mean ex-husband), but when I did get them and finally started taking feverfew every day, I noticed the frequency and intensity were greatly reduced.

DJ's Rx: Leave your mean husband/wife/partner/parent. Meanwhile, take feverfew capsules (50 to 100mg) daily.

The Spiral Staircase

Unending halls of darkness
filled with thumping and
shrieking. All exits are barred.

A staircase leads
nowhere I wish to go;
it spirals up to blinding light
or down to unspeakable
torture.

I hear a thumping
so loud it fills my ears and
tries to bore itself through
the center of my forehead.

The shrill winds rush within
my veins. In this castle
for the dark knights of the realm,
there is no escape.

We fight the dragon,
but we will never slay her.
I throw myself against the wall
like an espaliered pear tree,

my head shrinking
from the sharpened
knives of the second
day of migraine.

Remedy #12
From fellow migraineur Samantha:
Pinch the meat between your index finger and thumb up next to the bone. Hold it tight until your headache goes away.

Samantha's Rx: pinch between the index finger and thumb.

Hold Back the Dawn

Hold back the dawn; let me lie here
in this darkened cave of silence,
this unholy chamber lit only
by flickering blue aurora borealis
showing itself on the screens
covering my eyes.

The only sound, the throbbing
of blood in my spasming arteries.
My fingers cold, no matter how I clench
them inside the down blanket.

Nothing comforts me now. I breathe deeply,
imagine my spot at the beach on the island of St. John
where I go at times like these,
counting backward as I descend the stone steps
listening for the waves, waiting for the tide
to pull the pain from my head into the ocean.

The surf pounds in my forehead, the sun
streams through my window, as I reach
for my water bottle and pills.

Remedy #13
From my friend Kathay:

Take prescribed pain relief, and use gel ice packs on the neck.

Kathay's Rx: Medication as prescribed by your doctor. Gel ice packs on the back of your neck.

Two-Day Headache Binge

Okay, I admit it. I worked too much
last week. You are a jealous guardian
of my time. According to you
I have to sleep exactly the right amount
of time, eat exactly the right number
of meals, not too many calories,
never too few, watch the fats for god's sake,
and get enough water. Or else.

And we all know what *or else* means,
don't we? Me, all my friends, and anyone
who employed me in the last thirty years.

Oh, my god, if I don't obey your freaking rules
for one goddam minute. Do you have any idea
how sick and tired I am of this regimen?

As if I had a choice. No, no choice.
Too many hours worked last week,
so here you come with the sledgehammer, and
Bam!

Not just one day down. No. Today is Day Two.
Will I be allowed to work tomorrow?
Oh, pretty please, Master Migraine, you fucking
fuck?

Remedy #14
Give yourself an "ice cream" headache. Use chipped or crushed ice with a bit of water, and a straw to sip the ice water directly onto the roof of your mouth. Do this until your migraine stops.

Sandra's Rx: ice cream headache using ice and water.

Migraine Day Three

The third day of a migraine is
not like the first when lights
blind and sounds constantly increase
in volume until you want to shriek
and pound your head.

Nor is it like the second day
when the medicines failed.
Again. That day seems impossible;
the headache now wants out
instead of in to your head,
and you want to go home, to a home that
never was, and start your life over,
have a life that never ever includes headaches
of any kind, and especially
not migraines. Amen.

        Somehow—
probably with the help of your pills,
you get some sort of sleep that night.
Then you wake up, sure you will be
free of the bonds of pain.
You sit up, warily open your
eyes as wide as you're able, look around,
and realize that the migraine
is sitting right there. Right on your head.

        And this day,
this third day, there will be
no relief. No pills for you,

as they are for twice a week
only. And today, nothing
will work. Not ice, not rest,
not quiet, not self-hypnosis
or lavender or tea or crying
or laughing or anything else
except time.

Your forehead feels
as if it is bulging in and out like
a bellows, and your eyelids will
hang at half-mast. Until finally,
the storm breaks. You are free.
Until next time.

Remedy #15 Drugs

Sandra's Rx: Research shows that 80 percent of people with headache disorders have tried some form of alternative treatment, such as nutraceuticals. The most common nutraceuticals used for migraine prevention include magnesium, riboflavin (vitamin B2), and Coenzyme Q10 (CoQ10).

Another Migraine Poem

Monotonous, these migraines.
As in tiresome, fatiguing.
I am weary of entertaining the headaches.

They try to take up residence in my brain.
Even for a minute would now be too long.
I've grown bored of them;
they have lost all fascination, if they
ever had any.

They come with all their flash and glitter,
their pounding and throbbing, screaming and forcing
their way around as if they were
Hollywood's golden boys and girls.
I am quite over it.

Please begone.
Take your business elsewhere.
Find another head to spend your holidays,
and leave me in peace.

Remedy #16
From fellow migraineur Mandy:

I got a daith piercing in ear, and it's helped loads.

Mandy's Rx: Have a daith piercing in one or both ears. Some advocates of this piercing suggest it should be done to the ear on the side of your head where you feel the pain the most during a migraine. Daith piercing puts constant pressure on the vagus nerve, which then purportedly stimulates parts of the brain linked to migraine production.

The Lost Weekend

Another migraine, another no show.
Breaking appointments has become
the story of my life.

Not every weekend, not every day, but enough
that every time I lose a day or a weekend
or an event I held dear,

I know it went to my head
instead of to my memory banks.

How many friends have I lost to this malady?
Isn't it enough that I lost my job, disappointed
my children, my grandchildren
over and over *ad infinitum*
until they too began to enjoy the benefits
of this not so exclusive club of migraineurs?

Drawn curtains, dampened sounds,
multiple ice packs in the freezer
where once were popsicles,
medicine cabinets filled with remedies
rather than bottles of *eau de parfum*, which only
incites riots of nausea.

We wait impatiently
for the cure, which refuses
to come.

Remedy #17
From fellow migraineur Ann:

Butterbur works for my husband.

Ann's Rx:
Butterbur capsules, taken orally between 50 to 150mg daily.

People have used this plant for years to treat pain. Does it work to prevent migraines? When researchers looked at all the evidence, they found taking the extract reduced the number and intensity of headaches for some people.

To M

You are not welcome here.
I want time for other visitors.
and you are Nuisance.

I appreciate you left me alone
the entire month of January
this year; that was a true gift.

But February—a short month
—you surprised me on the sixth,
then came back on the eleventh,

again only a few days later,
and stayed for three whole days.
Now on the first day of March

here you are knocking on my
head in the middle of the afternoon,
acting like you are so happy to see me.

Got your spike heels on, stomping
around behind my eyes to some Taiko drum
you dragged along with you,

screaming how you like what I've done

with my frontal lobe, and poking
the cells with your nine-inch nails.

Why won't you leave me? I
asked you so many times.
I never loved you.

I haven't done you the violence
you've done me,
not to say I wouldn't.

If I could put a handle on you,
I would throw you somewhere
you could never hurt anyone
ever again.

Remedy #18 Magnesium

Sandra's Rx: Magnesium taken daily to reduce the number and severity of migraines. For at least three months, 400 mg daily.

Little Visits

Sometimes these little visits of yours
seem more unfair than other times.
Today for example.

I got up at 0530 to go to my extremely part-time job.
Love that job. And you know it, don't you?
Are you jealous of that?

I was so careful. Went to bed early,
got enough sleep. When I got to the job site,
I read all the ingredients on all the so-called breakfast items

to be certain none of my triggers rested on the snack table.
Well, there were hundreds there, but I didn't eat them. Not one.
No. I had a banana, a few almonds, coffee with real half and half.

That is all. Plenty of water. I even read the ingredient list
on the 100 percent ground coffee. Came home, ate my
breakfast of my usual, perfectly safe food.

Relaxed, did my writing, my reading, my housework,
prepared for my Italian class. And thirty minutes

before I was to leave:
Kaboom!

Here you are, knocking on my head.
Pulling the rug out from under any fun
I had planned for my evening.
No way. Why? Why?

Remedy #19
From my friend Kate:

If ice doesn't cause the ache to subside, I brew 3/4 cup water with a teabag (green tea) for 3 minutes (cooling it down with an ice cube once it's brewed) and drink this with one regular Tylenol and one regular aspirin. I take these three things together.

Kate's Rx: Brew for three minutes three-fourths cup of water with green tea, and drink while taking one Tylenol, and one aspirin.

Migraines Might Slow You Down

People say:
"I can't believe how productive you are."
"I can't believe you get so much done even when you have migraines!"
"How do you do it all?"
"Where do you find the time?"

You know the adage: if you do what you love, you'll never work a day in your life?
I worked all my life at day jobs
in order to have a pension to allow me to
work full-time at what I was already doing part-time.

Now I produce more than ever.
The minute I began to write full-time,
turn my attention to my own work,
my life became my own.
Why would I shirk what I love?

Migraines slow me down. A lot.
They haven't stopped me.

Remedy #20
From my friend Katy:

I'm on monthly Aimovig shots, which block some information in the dura and are prescribed for migraines. Mine also respond to bracing, neck support, and caffeine. I spend a lot of my time in dark rooms with no music, well supported on pillows to control my migraines. I have a variety of typical creams and scalp oil to keep the neck pain down, so it doesn't escalate. My neck is almost constantly on ice. I also use a ginger powder drink from Trader Joe's, Chinese Skullcap, and feverfew to try to chip away at it.

Katy's Rx: Aimovig injection, monthly. For breakthrough migraine headaches, apply bracing, neck support, and drink caffeine. Lie in a dark room, well supported by pillows, no music. Apply creams and scalp oil for neck pain. Use ice on the neck. Take a ginger powder drink from Trader Joe's, Chinese Skullcap, and feverfew capsules.

[The poet suggests you check with your naturopath for prescriptions, and your MD or neurologist for Aimovig prescription.]

A True Story by A. Migraineur

The truth of a migraine is
blinding pain. Throbbing pain
on one side or the other, or
in the forehead. The truth is
one feels like she might die of a
headache, and then she does not.

The burden of migraineurs is
one is subject to the whims of a
headache that takes away the
appetite and replaces it with
doubt you will ever again be a
reliable person.

There are no cures for migraine, only
guesses mixed with derision. What works
for one will not help another.
What works for another may help only
once or twice.

The bad days are given over to writhing,
crying, and begging for relief.
One savors the good days with a
bowl of gratitude soup.

Remedy #21
From my friend Jill:

Botox, and for breakthrough migraines, loads of Tylenol, a sinus OTC med, and if it's scary bad, I add a prescribed painkiller.

Jill's Rx: Botox. Tylenol, 1000 mg every four hours. Over-the-counter sinus medicine, as directed.

The Worst

The worst part of having a migraine
is not the pain
not the light sensitivity
not the way everything sounds too loud.

The worst part of having a migraine is
not that you can't sleep
or think
or concentrate.

It isn't that you can't read
or watch television
or listen to the radio
or stand your neighbors.

It isn't even that you don't feel
like making your bed,
getting dressed,
having a shower.

Nor is it that you wish
your cat would get its own dinner
scoop its own box
do nothing but provide comfort.

No. The worst thing about having a migraine is
everyone has a cure, and they
will share it with you, whether or not
you want to hear it.

Remedy #22
From me, Sandra de Helen:
See your doctor, naturopath, neurologist, whomever you see for your headaches, and if your migraines are chronic, ask for monthly injections of CGRP inhibitors. What are CGRP inhibitors? Calcitonin gene-related peptide (CGRP) inhibitors block the effect of CGRP, which is a small protein that is highly prevalent in the sensory nerves that supply the head and the neck. CGRP is involved in pain transmission, and levels increase during a migraine attack.

I started with monthly injections of Aimovig. After a year or so, Kaiser Permanente switched me to Emgality. There are many other brands of this injection. Also available are CGRP inhibitor pills for breakthrough or acute migraine attacks. These have not worked for me, but apparently they work for the tennis sensation Serena Williams.

Sandra's Rx: Calcitonin gene-related peptide inhibitors. Ask your doctor for CGRP injections and/or pills. Search the internet for a list of brand names available.

Afterword

The condition of migraine is physical. Migraine is a genetic neurologic disease. Because the primary symptom is a headache, there is a lot of stigma around migraine.

Migraine is common. It affects one in five women, one in sixteen men, even one in eleven children. Migraine attacks are three times more prevalent in women.

Because migraine is genetic, it is hereditary. If a parent has migraine, the offspring have a fifty percent chance of also having it.

This collection of poetry was written to honor all those who suffer from migraine and the suggested remedies.

About the Author

Sandra de Helen published her first poem at the age of fourteen. Her English teacher, Janice Wallace, submitted the poem to a teacher's magazine and surprised Sandra with a copy in print. The poem was about abortion, which was illegal at the time (and may be again soon in this country).

In her twenties, Sandra published a few poems in newspapers, which spurred her to take a Creative Writing Class at the local community college. The [male] professor predicted she would never make a good poet because she didn't "write like a man." The next year she joined the women's movement and turned to writing plays.

Forty years later, she picked up Sage Cohen's book, *Writing the Life Poetic: An Invitation to Read and Write Poetry*, and resumed writing poems like a woman. Sandra also writes novels, essays, theater reviews, and a weekly newsletter.

Sandra is a long-time resident of Portland, Oregon, where she lives with her daughter, chickens, and cats.

Other Books in the Poetry for the New Millennium Series

From Launch Point Press by
Sandra de Helen

I Eat My Words:
Poetry and Recipes (2022)

The World's a Stage:
Life in Five Acts (2021)

Poetry for the People:
Heavy Verse (2020)

Lesbian Humor is Not an Oxymoron:
Light Verse (2019)

Desire Returns for a Visit:
Intimate Poems about Lesbian Love (2018)

Note to Readers

Thank you for reading a book from Launch Point Press. We have made every effort to edit this book. However, typos do slip in. If you find an error in the text, please email publisher@launchpointpress.com so the issue can be corrected.

We appreciate you as a reader and want to ensure you enjoy the reading process. We would like you to consider posting a review on your preferred media sites and/or your blog or website.

For more information on upcoming releases, author interviews, contests, giveaways and more, please sign up for our newsletter and visit us as at Launch Point Press: www.launchpointpress.com and "Like" us on Facebook: Launch Point Press.

Bright Blessings